What's Left of Me

What's Left of Me

An English and Arabic
Poetry Collection

Nora Elsayed

Copyright © 2023 Nora Elsayed
All rights reserved.
ISBN: 9798218291983

DEDICATION

To my mother, Amani Mohammed, one day I hope to be half the mother you are to me. Thank you for giving up your dreams and your family to support my dreams and build our family. To my father, Yasier Elsayed, the sound of the oud you played and Arabic music you sang that filled our home was my introduction to poetry. Thank you for embracing a country you didn't know and raising me to take full advantage of it. To my siblings, Hassan and Fatma Elsayed, you both never failed to challenge and support me. I'm lucky to have you by my side for life. To the rest of my aunts, uncles, cousins, and village of a family, you all played a part in raising me whether we were neighbors or miles apart. Thank you for never allowing me to be alone.

To my chosen family from UNC-Chapel Hill, Richard Montgomery High School, Shady Grove Middle School, Flower Hill Elementary School and everyone I've met along my way, you all inspire me every single day. Thank you for giving me the priceless love of friendship.

A special thank you to Yasin Mohammed Yasin, for his time in helping me translate and edit the Arabic poems, because of you I am able to share my writing with my family all over the world.

Finally, to my beautiful country of Sudan, I dedicate my entire life to representing you well. Thank you for making me who I am. May you come back from every moment of adversary stronger and more united than ever.

AUTHOR'S NOTE

Often, I hear from others about how *lucky* I am in life and I can't help but agree. My entire life I have been sacrificed for, loved, supported, and encouraged. I wouldn't trade a second of it for anything in the world. But as life persistently demonstrates, luck eventually wears thin, and we find ourselves ensnared in the clutches of the inevitable misery.

The "evil eye" represents an unseen malice that dances in jealous eyes, casting an unwitting curse upon the unsuspecting soul. Often worn or displayed, the circular blue symbol protects against this malice gaze.

The symbolism and essence of the evil eye have always resonated deeply with me, becoming a tangible representation of the fortune in my life. I wear it around my neck as a daily reminder. In fact, if you were to step into my room or my car, you'd notice its ubiquitous presence. So, when the time came to design the cover of this book that celebrates my charmed existence, the evil eye naturally emerged as the clear choice. Every life moment highlighted in this book, good or bad, is a reminder of that the good fortune I am given and the good fortune I hope continues.

This collection of poetry has been a long time in the making. As I sit here, writing these words at 3:57 PM on May 31st, halfway across the world in Thailand, I still can't fathom the fact that I'm actually releasing this book. I'm not sure if it's fear or excitement that fuels this disbelief, but either way, it's hard to envision what my life will be like, holding a tangible copy of every emotion and experience, etched as cold, unyielding text. The thought of others interpreting my work only amplifies the intensity of this sentiment. All the poems contained within this collection have been cherished and guarded closely, like sacred treasures, for an extended period. Some, remarkably vulnerable and personal, have become sanctuaries where I seek solace, revisiting them to validate my own thoughts. Others serve as outlets, allowing me to unburden myself, furiously typing away my anger and fueling my self pity. I can't pinpoint the precise moment when I decided it was time to release these poems, but at some point, the notion of "letting go" materialized in the form of this book. Honestly, I think I wanted the poems to take me on a new adventure. Dwelling on them and rereading them became boring and I knew they had the potential for something else. So now, I look forward to seeing the ways my poems transform in the eyes of someone else. The myriad of meanings each reader extracts, the diverse applications they find, and even the criticism they may encounter. I don't expect my poems, emotions, and experiences to resonate with everyone who reads them, but my hope is they take something from it.

The title, "What's Left of Me" came from this sentiment too. It seemed to be the perfect phrase to encompass the idea of "letting go" and giving away the one thing I had left for me to keep private.

I also knew if I'm going to be sharing these experiences about my life publicly then it's only fair that those closest to me can understand it as well, hence why its written in both Arabic and English. My first and second languages.

I'd be remiss if I didn't give one last thanks to the hidden authors of this book—the individuals whom I have written about.

To those obvious, and those not so obvious, thank you. Your time and impact on my life have left an indelible mark, deserving of an entire page within the written collection of my youth. I took great pride in immortalizing the people I hold most dear and conveying their influence on me through these pages. Each one of their poems represents a stretched out version of "I love you".

On the other hand, to the ambiguous poems I wrote about others, it's quite beautiful how a tragic situation can at the very least gift us with a compelling story, and an even better poem. Although these less obvious poems do not center on a particular person, I encourage you to perceive them as representatives of a common societal figure. Let these poems embody whoever you, the reader, wish them to represent and if the shoe fits, by all means, wear it.

Finally, I want to say from the bottom of my heart, a **big** thank you to the person holding this book right now that have spent their hard earned money to purchase it. This has been a dream to create and a dream to share.

If there is one piece of advice I can give you, it would be to please **write more**. Write about your love, your hate, your misfortunes, your luck, your enviable disappointments and your eventual successes. You owe it to yourself to show those after you that you've lived. Writing is our only way of freezing time, it is magical and it is limitless. I urge you to take advantage of its magic and write more. Maybe you'll find yourself up at 3 AM one day frantically searching your documents and downloads for old poems to include in a book you randomly had the idea to create.

Now, I hope you enjoy this. Dive into its pages, get lost in its words, and hopefully, you'll find a piece of yourself in here too.

Much love and gratitude,

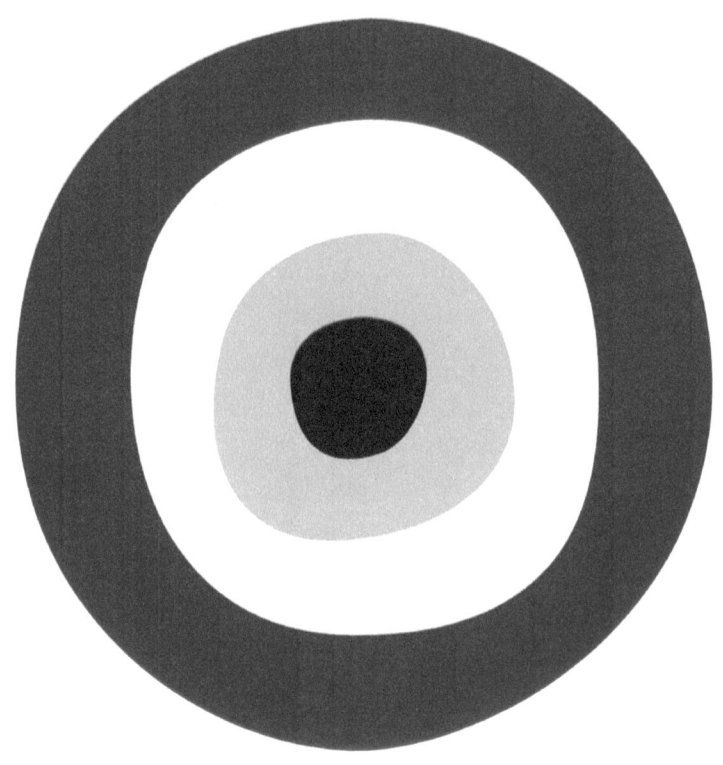

x

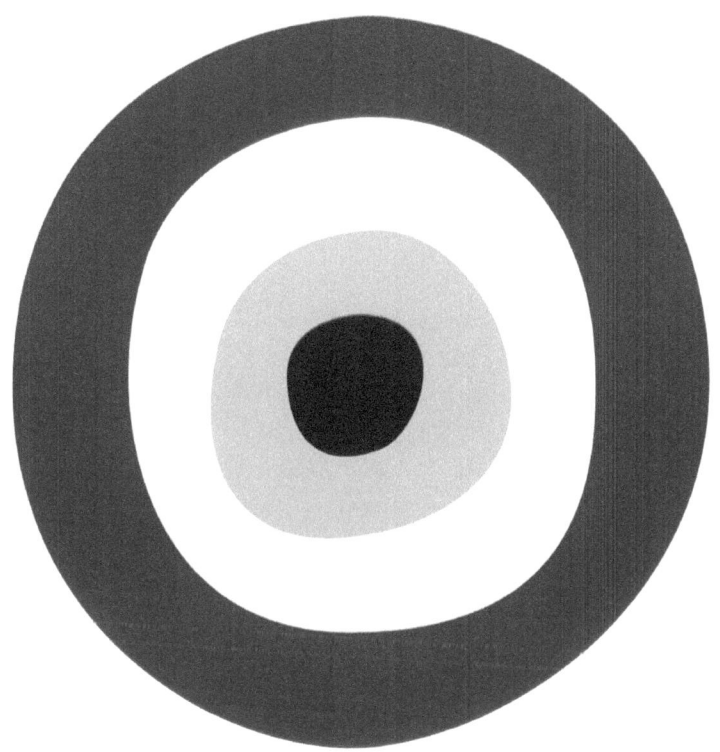

خريطة

عندما يصبح من الصعب استخدام كلماتي

أبدأ في التفكير في أفكاري في الثالث

في الثامن ، في السادس عشر

في آلات البيانو أو الطبول

تصبح الأوتار كلمات في نظام تحديد المواقع العالمي

نقل الشعور إلى عنوانه الخاص

Map

When it becomes hard to use my words

I start thinking of my thoughts in thirds

In 8ths, in 16ths

In pianos or drums

Chords become words in a GPS

Transporting a feeling into its own address

What's Left of Me

بعد

ما إذا كنت سأموت لأبقى بلا روح في جسدي

مطرزة بشكل دائم في العالم

آمل أن يسمح لي بالحفاظ على الضوء الذي أشعل بداخلي

سواء كنت سأموت وأعيش وسط الوقت الذي يدير فيه عالمنا

دعوت لأتذكر الزهرة التي خرجت من ظلام التراب

لأنه في بعض الأيام بدا الأمر وكأنه الشيء الوحيد الذي انتظرته

البتلة التي قد تنبت

قد ينبت هذا إذا انتظرت طويلاً بما فيه الكفاية

What's Left of Me

After

Whether I'd die to remain soulless in a body permanently

embroidered within the world

I hope He lets me keep the light that sparked within me

Whether I'd die and live amongst the time that runs our world

I prayed to remember the flower that emerged from the

darkness of dirt

because some days it seemed like the only thing I waited for

The petal that might sprout

That might sprout if I waited long enough

فضول

عندما تصبح حماستي لمغادرة العالم دائمة

أعتقد أنني سأطلب المساعدة

لكن حماسي يأتي بدلاً من ذلك من وباء يسمى الفضول

أنا فقط أسميها طاعون لأنه قادني إلى أبواب مغلقة

اعتقدت الأبواب كانت مفتوحة ولكن من الداخل ملوثة

على الرغم من ذلك يجب أن أكون سعيدة

لأنني ما كان يجب أن أذهب على أي حال

ولكن ماذا لو أردت ذلك ،

الإغراء الذي استدعى الفضول

Curiosity

When my excitement to soon leave the world becomes

permanent

I think I'll seek help

But my excitement comes instead from a plague called curiosity

Only I call it a plague because it has led me to 'X' marked doors

Doors I thought were open but inside infected

I should be happy though

because I shouldn't have gone in anyway

But what if I wanted to,

the temptress that compelled curiosity

اثنان

أغنيتان منفصلتان بنفس الإيقاع من خلالهما

عقلان منفصلان ولكن كان الحب بداخل واحد فقط

أتمنى أن تكون قد عرفت كيف شعرت من خلالها

لأنه على الرغم من أنني أعتقد أنه يجب عليك القيام بذلك

لقد تحركت ضده بشكل أعمى تقريبًا

Two

Two separate songs with the same beat through it

Two separate minds but only one had love in it

I wish that you'd known how I felt through it

because although I think you should've

You moved almost blindly against it

المحصورة

كل جمال العالم رأيته في عينيك

وهم يلتفون ضد أنفسهم مثل موجة المياه تلتقي

مع كل هبة ريح ، كانت تتألق بصوت أعلى

لم أحب المحيط أبدًا وكل ما يحيط به من عدم المجهول

لكنني أعجبت بك وكل غموضك

الطريقة التي أبقيتني مقيدًا بها في وسطها

مثل رسالة مغلفة في زجاجة مجوفة

لأنه في نهاية بحر من عدم المجهول

هناك احتمال أن يفهم شخص ما اللغز

Bounded

All the beauty in the world I saw in your eyes

As they curled against themselves like a wave meeting water

With every gust of wind, they only gleamed louder

I never liked the ocean and all of its uncertainty

But I liked you and all of your mystery

The way you've kept me bound in the midst of it

Like an encapsulated message in the hollow bottle

because at the end of a sea of uncertainty

There's a possibility that someone will understand the mystery

الهروب

دموعك تريد الهروب

ابقي السجين في قضبان جفنك

يحكمها دماغك الذي لا هوادة فيه

بقلب مصنوع من الفولاذ وعلى شكل مفتاح

لكنهم أبرياء

الاقرار بالذنب وبحق

لكن هيئة محلفين أعمياء من الخوف

مع قاض لا يرحم

أرسلهم بعيدًا مدى الحياة دون فرصة للإفراج المشروط

مكبل اليدين بسرعة ومطلي باللون البرتقالي

حتى داخل

شريط الصلب شرطة

وجدت دموعك مهربًا

Escape

Your tears want to escape

Kept prisoner in your eyelid bars

Policed by your relentless brain

With a heart made of steel and key-shaped

But they are innocent

Pleading guilty and rightfully so

But a blinded jury of fear

With a merciless judge

Sent them away for life with no chance of parole

Quickly handcuffed and painted in orange

Even within

Bar policed steel

Your tears found an escape

What's Left of Me

أنت

بطريقة ما كنت لا تزال قادرا على محاصرتي

مخنوق بالكلمات التي أريد أن أقولها

لكن توقفت من عند تلك التي لم تفعلها ابدا

إذا كنت فقط تستطيع استعارة عيني لهذا اليوم

ربما قلبي البالي سوف يتجدد

يمكنك أن ترى الطريقة التي أراك بها

أو حبني كما فعلت

لأنني أحببتك بما يكفي لأفقد نفسي

وأنت تحبني بما يكفي لاستخدام نفسي

You

Somehow you still manage to surround me

Choked up by the words I want to say

but stopped by the ones you never did

If only you could borrow my eye for the day

Maybe my worn-out heart will refurbish

You could see the way I see you

or love me the way I did

Because I loved you enough to lose myself

and you loved me enough to use myself

ذهب

الأحلام الذهبية لا تصدأ مثل السوار الذي اعطيتني

أو تكذب بكلمات شفافة

لكني احتفظت به

لأنه حتى مع لونه القديم

سأتذكره دائمًا على أنه ذهب

لامع ومشرق

يمكن تحقيقه وحفظه

لي امد بعيد

أو انتظر ، ذاك ؟

Gold

Golden dreams don't rust like the bracelet you got me

or lie with transparent words

But I kept it

because even with its old color

I'll always remember it as gold

As shiny and bright

Attainable and secure

Long-lasting and captivating

Or wait, was that you?

الوقت الخطأ ، المكان المثالي

أعزف مثل أغنية عيد الميلاد في الربيع

أو بيت صيفي في الشتاء

حب سام لدرجة أنه بدا وكأنه لمسة من الله

شاهد يهوه او المسيح هكذا

أفرغت الأمتعة التي بحوزتي

لتأخذ مالك بدلا عنها

لذلك يمكن لقلبك الحر أن يقود الطريق

لأن قلبي يحتاج إلى وقت

ليتجدد ويصبح العلامة التجارية الجديدة

أنت فقط لا تعرف

الي اي مدي اقتربت من الشمس لاجلك

إيكاروس بأجنحة مكسورة

دمية تحركها أوتار قلبها

Wrong Time, Perfect Place

I play like a Christmas song in the spring

or a summer house in the winter

A love so supreme it almost seemed like god's touch

A Jehovah's witness or Christ such

I emptied the luggage I held for me

to take yours in instead

So your free heart can lead the way

because mine needs time

To refurbish and become brand new

You just don't know

How close I flew to the sun for you

An Icarus with broken wings

A puppet moved by her heartstrings

Look at Where You Are

Who said with time I'll heal

A compelling lie

It only seems to be getting worse

The longing hurts

The waiting's expensive

My money is all gone

Wasted on you

Colored with blue

It all lies here now

Marked with scattered headstones on a lawn

The pretty green lawn

We all end up the same

Even those with broken hearts

or empty promises

Those who went too early

or got caught in waiting

What's Left of Me

Dirt piled on hurt bodies

Left for its bone and skull

Paralleled the way you left me

Unattached and no source of stream

Maybe my heart will compost

Maybe these feelings will go with it too

Finally, they'll find themselves in earth

with everything else I've been through

انظر إلى مكان وجودك

من قال مع الوقت سأشفى

كذبة قاهرة

ويبدو أنها تزداد سوءا

الشوق يؤلم

الانتظار مكلف

لقد ذهبت أموالي كلها الآن

ضاعت من اجلك

بلون أزرق

كل شيء موجود هنا الآن

تنتشر شواهد القبور على العشب

عشب أخضر جميل

كلنا ننتهي بنفس الشيء

حتى أولئك الذين يعانون من كسر القلوب

أو وعود فارغة

أولئك الذين ذهبوا مبكرا جدا

أو معلقين

What's Left of Me

تراكم الأوساخ على الجثث المصابة

غادر لعظمته وجمجمته

إنه يوازي الطريقة التي تركتني بها

مبتور ولا يوجد مصدر حالي
ربما يتسمد قلبي

ربما هذه المشاعر تتماشى معها أيضًا

أخيرًا ، سوف يجدون أنفسهم في الأرض

مع كل ما مررت به

أربعة جدران

انظر إلى هذا المنزل المؤقت الذي بنيناه

الواجهة التي أنشأناها سويا

يداها حمراء في دمائها

ضحيتان للجريمة

انظر إلى أنك مغطي بكل ذنبها

من منبوذ ومنأسف يرقص تحت جماله الزائف

أقدام تتحرك على الخشب البني المزيت

تلمس الأيدي لتشتيت الانتباه عن الكلمات التي لم تقال

هذه اللحظات كانت مخصصة للمنزل

4 Walls

Look at this temporary house we built

The facade we both created

Hands dripped red in its blood

Two victims of crime

Look at you covered in all its guilt

of a renounced and regretted that danced under its false beauty

Feet shifting on the oiled brown wood

Hands touching to distract from unsaid words

These moments were meant for a home

What's Left of Me

في هذا الموسم

قلب بارد يبحث عن الابتسامات الدافئة

لكن لم تترك أي زهور جميلة

لم يأت نحل العسل ليجمع

أصبح منزلنا المؤقت الآن بمفرده

الدموع الهاربة هطلت حتى نمت

وتركه لمن يسمونه قريبًا بالمنزل

In This Season

An ice-cold heart looking for warm smiles

But no pretty flowers were left

No honey bees came to collect

Our temporary house is now left alone

Escaped tears watered till it's grown

and left it for those who'd soon call it home

اختيار

جاءت الشجيرات المثالية من بستانيين مدفوعة

والأكاذيب الكاملة جاءت من الحقائق الخفية

أحيانًا يكون الأكثر شرًا فينا

يخرج في لحظات نقائنا

حب منبوذ من جزء من الشباب

لقد استخدمت ذلك عذرا

كاسبابك للانتظار

لماذا أكتب كل هذه البلوز

إذا كنت تستطيع رسم حبي

ما اللون الذي تختاره

أو ما هو الموسم الذي تريده؟

Paletted Pick

Perfect bushes come from paid gardeners

and perfect lies come from hidden truths

Sometimes the most evil in us

come out in our moments of purity

A forsaken love that's a part of youth

I used that as your excuse

as your reasons for waiting

Why I'm writing all these blues

If you could paint my love

What color would you choose

or what season would you cue?

يدفع

نحن نعيش في عالم مادي

حيث اصبح حبك عملة

باهتمام غير مدفوع الأجر

لماذا لا يمكن مجانا

لماذا يكلفني الكثير

Paid Off

We live in a monetary world

Where even your love's a currency

With unpaid attention

Why can't it just be free

Why does it cost so much of me

What's Left of Me

انظر لي بحرية

في بعض الأحيان أرغب في الحصول على بشرة شفافه

لأهرب من الألم الذي جلبه لي هذا الشخص

الاهتمام الذي أخذته مني

أو أعطيته لي

إذا كان بإمكان الناس فقط النظر من خلالي

يمكنهم أن يروا ما بداخلي

أخيراً،

انظر لي

See Me Freely

Sometimes I'd wish for translucent skin

to run away from the pain this one brought me

The attention it has taken from me

or given me

If people could just look through me

They can see in me

Finally,

See Me

My First Meeting with Grief

I never really knew her

The woman who gave me my life

I just knew her from the reflection she cast upon my mother

I knew her warm smile

Her welcoming eyes

I knew her phrases

Her rules

I lived with the extension of her,

the extension that held me in her womb

But I wish I knew her

The source that created the one that created me

Now I just blame myself for her departure

Could I have moved time faster?

If I worked a little harder?

Could I have let my mother hold hers one more time?

Did I take away that warm smile?

or those welcoming eyes?

I don't think I'll ever know

What's Left of Me

because I'm not sure if next time I'll see that mother

If she'll hug her tighter

or picture me regret

Because the life she bought me

cost so much of hers

Was it worth it

Mother?

لقائي الأول مع الحزن

لم أكن أعرفها حقًا

المرأة التي أعطتني حياتي

لقد عرفتها من التأمل الذي ألقته على والدتي

عرفت ابتسامتها الدافئة

عيناها المرحبتين

عرفت عباراتها

قواعدها

، عشت مع امتداد لها

الامتداد الذي حبسني في بطنها

لكني تمنيت لو كنت أعرفها

المصدر الذي أنشأني

الآن أنا فقط ألوم نفسي على رحيلها

هل استطيع تحريك الوقت بشكل أسرع؟

إذا عملت بجد أكثر؟

هل كان بإمكاني أن اجعل والدتي تمسك بها مرة أخرى؟

هل أخذت تلك الابتسامة الدافئة؟

أو تلك العيون المرحبة ؟

What's Left of Me

لا أعتقد أنني سأعرف أبدًا

لأنني لست متأكدًا ان كنت سأرى تلك الأم في المرة القادمة

إذا كانت ستعانقها بقوة

أو صورت لي الندم

لأنها التي جلبتها لي الحياة

كلفها الكثير من راتبها

هل كان يستحق

امي؟

الازدواجية

الشيء الوحيد الذي يبقينا بشر

الطريقة التي يحب بها جسدنا عقولنا

تفاعلاتهم

اتصالاتهم

جهد مشترك لتوليف ما يجري في الخارج

غالبًا ما أذكر نفسي بأنني موجود

لأنني فقدت المرساة المقيدة إلى كاحلي

الآن الأرض هربت من أسفل قدمي

بدلا من ذلك أشعر كل يوم انني طافية

مع أحلام جرفت على حافة الشاطئ

أريد عقلي أن يقع في حب جسدي مرة أخرى

أحتاجهم للتصالح

لإعادة ربط المرساة التي أبعدتني

قبل أن أدخل هذا الفراغ ولا أجد نفسي بعد الآن

لا أعرف ماذا أفعل بدونها

Duality

The only thing that keeps us human

The way our body loves our mind

Their interactions

Their communications

A conjoined effort to synthesize what's going on outside

I'd often remind myself that I'm present

because I lost the anchor tied down to my ankle

Now the ground escapes the bottom of my feet

Instead every day I feel afloat

With washed-up dreams at the edge of the shore

I need my mind to fall in love with my body again

I need them to reconcile

To retie the anchor that kept me down

Before I enter this void and can't find myself anymore

I don't know what I'd do without her

انسكاب

عندما يبدا الالم في الانسكاب

أشعر بالعقل المذعور يخربش لإغلاقه

أشعر بأكاذيب وابتسامة زائفة

أشعر بصدمات في القلب وارتعاش اليد

أدرك أن تغمض عينيك هو جمال تم تجاهله

، عندما ترتاح جفوننا على خدودنا ويتوقف العالم بإرادتك

فعندئذ فقط يمكنك السماح لهم بالرجوع

هل تفتح عينيك وتواجه الألم مرة أخرى؟

Spill

When the pain beings to spill

I feel the panicked mind scrabble to close it

I feel the patched lies and fake smile

I feel heart jolts and hand shakes

I realize to close your eyes is a beauty that's gone overlooked

When our lids rest over our cheeks and the world stops at your will,

then only at your power do you let them back in

Do you open your eyes and face the pain again?

مكواة

أحيانًا اكتوي لأشعر بالقرب من والدتي

بينما أشمر عن أكمام معطفي المزوّد بسحاب

تومض الصور الموازية لها في ذهني

الطيات المعقدة كل قطعة من الملابس تحمل علامة تجارية

كما أنها تمسك بآلة البخار الثقيلة ضدهم

المهام المنزلية الغريبة التي يتعلمها الأطفال المهاجرون

أولئك الذين لم يتركهم آباؤنا مطلقًا

أولئك الذين كرهناهم يكبرون لأن عقولنا الغربية أرادت التحرر منهم

لكننا الآن نجلس وحدنا

كما يفعل آباؤنا في المنزل

لأنهم يفعلون ذلك ليشعروا بالقرب من أمهاتهم

الذين تركوا لنا

The Iron

Sometimes I iron to feel closer to my mother

As I roll up the sleeves of my zippered hoodie

The parallel images of her flash through my mind

The intricate folds each piece of clothing is branded

As she brushes the steam heavy instrument against them

The weird domestic tasks immigrant children learn

The ones our parents never let go off

The ones we hated growing up because our western minds

wanted free of them

But now we sit alone

As our parents at home do them

Because they do it to feel closer to their moms

The ones they left for us

ما الذي يمكنك أخذه أيضًا؟

لا يمكنك إزالة عيني ، ما زلت أقع في الحب

لا يمكنك إزالة أذني ، ما زلت أقع في الحب

لا يمكنك حتى إزالة قلبي ، ما زلت أقع في الحب

عليك إزالة روحي

لذا سأحتاج أولاً أن أجد نفسي ثم أقع في الحب

What's Left of Me

What Else Can You Take?

You can't remove my eyes, I'd still fall in love

You can't remove my ears, I'd still fall in love

You can't even remove my heart, I'd still fall in love

You'd have to remove my soul

So first I'd need to find myself and then I'd fall in love

تحدث

الهواء من حولنا مليء بالكلمات التي لن نقولها أبدًا

اللمحات هي المحادثات الوحيدة التي نجريها

وأعيننا تحكي قصص ما كنا عليه

Conversate

The air around us is thick with words we'd never say

Glances are the only conversations we hold

and our eyes tell the stories of what we were

Elsayed

I don't think anyone will know me better than the tiles of my kitchen floor
I skated across them empowered by the misery of my own emotions
The people that felt like statues engraved on those tiles I missed
I miss the man that sat in the woven chairs mimicking his old life
The song that his fingers strung out of the wooden instrument
I would forget all of the beauty I'd seen to listen to it one more time
To hear the words he'd traced from his personified emotions
But I miss the women that stood on the other side of him
I mentioned her earlier,
the statue
She held us together through the flavor she'd curate
The ones magnified by flames or sliced by metal
Ingredients she didn't need to measure
All these fancy ways to describe her food
I miss the other two
The one who never stopped speaking
She kept us on our toes
The youngest that made me remember how fun it is to forget your living
How warm it felt to move so freely with the beat trailing you

What's Left of Me

But now I feel so cold

I shiver constantly

I shift frequently

Never quite sitting correctly

because the statue of our house isn't holding it any longer

We are stuck with this temporary glue

and the man in the woven chair doesn't sing to us

I barely see him anymore

He tries to make up for the ones that aren't here but now he isn't either

and the one with the moving mouth has gone silent

I think I wished for her to be quiet too much

Now I feel so alone

Like I hold the memories of what our house once was

The music that rang from its walls

Our paint feels dull

Our furniture unused

Our words stale

It doesn't work when we aren't all together

I forgot how fast lives move

But you remember when it starts to get picked apart

I hope this ends soon

What's Left of Me

السيد

لا أعتقد أن أحداً سيعرفني أكثر من بلاط

أرضية مطبخنا

لقد تزلجت عبرهم بفضل بؤس مشاعري

الأشخاص الذين شعروا وكأنهم تماثيل محفورة على ذاك البلاط افتقدتهم

أفتقد الرجل الذي جلس على الكراسي المنسوج يحاكي حياته الاولي

الأغنية التي اخرجتها أصابعه من الآلة الخشبية

سانسي كل الجمال الذي رايته لاستمع اليه

لسماع الكلمات التي تنبع من مشاعره الشخصية

لكني أفتقد النساء اللواتي وقفن على الجانب الآخر منه

، لقد ذكرتها من قبل

التمثال

لقد جمعتنا معًا من خلال النكهة التي كانت ترعاها

تلك المكبرة بالنيران أو المقطعة بالمعدن

المكونات التي لم تكن بحاجة للقياس

كل هذه الطرق الفاخرة لوصف طعامها

اشتاق الاثنين الاخرين

الشخص الذي لم يتوقف عن الكلام

لقد أبقتنا على الامشاط

الأصغر الذي جعلني أتذكر كم هو ممتع لينسيك معيشتك

كم شعرت بالدفء وأنت تتحرك بحرية مع الإيقاع الذي يتخلف عنك

What's Left of Me

لكني الآن أشعر بالبرد الشديد

أنا أرتجف باستمرار

أنا اتغير بشكل متكرر

لا تجلس بشكل صحيح

لأن تمثال منزلنا لم يعد ممسكًا به

نحن عالقون مع هذا الغراء المؤقت

والرجل الذي في الكرسي المنسوج لم يعد يغني لنا بعد الآن

لم اعد أراه بعد الآن

يحاول تعويض الأشخاص غير الموجودين هنا ولكنه الآن ليس كذلك

اصبح صامتا

عتقد أنني تمنيت لها أن تكون هادئة أكثر من اللازم

الآن أشعر بالوحدة

كأنني أحتفظ بذكريات ما كان عليه منزلنا في يوم من الأيام

الموسيقى التي عزفت في جدرانه

الطلاء لدينا يشعر بالملل

أثاثنا غير مستخدم

كلماتنا التي لا معنى لها

لا يعمل عندما لا نكون جميعًا معًا

لقد نسيت كيف تتحرك الحياة بسرعة

لكنك تتذكر عندما يبدأ في التفتت

آمل أن ينتهي هذا قريبا

الفاكهة المحرمة

لا أستطيع التعرف على هذا الشخص الذي جعلتني أكون عليه

الإمساك الذي أبقيت عليّ من كلامك فقط

يا الله أكتب القصائد

أعرف قوة الرسائل المنسقة المرتبطة ببعضها البعض

لكني ما زلت مندهشة هذه المرة

ما مدى قربك من الألغام

كيف بدوا قريبين وكأنهم يربطون بنفس الطريقة

بنفس الترتيب

أنت لا تلتقي بهذه الأنواع عادة

لكن بالطبع ما ألتقي به يصبح فاكهتي الممنوعة

التفاحة لا أستطيع ابتلاعها ولكنها كانت قريبة جدًا من وجهي

طريقة قريبة جدا

Forbidden Fruit

I can't recognize this person you've made me be

The grasp you kept on me from only your words

God, I write poems

I know the power of curated letters tied together

But I still got surprised this time

How close yours were to mine

How they seemed to tie in the same fashion

with the same order

You don't meet those types usually

But of course the one I do becomes my own forbidden fruit

The apple I can't swallow but held so close to my face

Way too close

كل شيء وحوض الحمام

أغلقت عقلي بينما لا تزال الأفكار تتساقط مثل الصنبور

المجموعة الضئيلة منهم تتجول داخل جسدي

يبحثون عن استنزاف سوف يدخلون

لكني أعتقد أنهم ضلوا طريقهم

يبدو أن الإفراج عنهم قد أغلق

لذا فإن الأفكار تبقى خارجا

مرتجفة وباردة

Everything and the Bathroom Sink

I shut my mind while thoughts still drip like a faucet

The tiny collection of them roaming amongst my body

Looking for the drain they'll enter

But I think they've lost their way

The release they once had seems closed

So the thoughts stay out

Shivered and cold

قصة

أناشد مع الوقت لأغفر لك

لذلك سيكون لديك المزيد منه

لأن إخفاقات ماضيك خدرتك

الآن لا يمكن أن يلمسك الوقت

لا تشعر انه يتحرك

أنت ترى الناس يغادرون فقط

لقد أصبح اختفائهم بمثابة كوب قياس خاص بك للساعة

تتحرك اليد الصغيرة وفقًا لأكبرها

لو أخبرتك الحياة بأنك ستحصل على ثانية واحدة أخرى

أين ستضعها؟

Storyline

I plead with time to forgive you

So you'd have more of it

Because the failures of your past have numbed you

Now time can't touch you

You don't feel it moving

You just see people leaving

Their disappearance have become your own measuring cup of a clock

The little hand moves in accordance to its eldest

If life had told you that you'd get one more second

Where would you place it?

أصدقاء ليلة الجمعة

الضحك طريقتي الملتوية للدموع

فمي يحول صرخات النجدة إلى نكات تذوب

كالجدار الصلب يستسلم للنار ويبكي

تحول أذني الصدمات التي جمعتها إلى رسومات كوميدية لأصدقاء ليلة الجمعة

لذلك كانوا يصفعون على ركبهم ويجعدون عيونهم

فتنهار جباههم وتتسع أفواههم

لذلك كانوا يمسكون بطونهم ويقبضون اكفهم

غريب كيف ينظرون في لحظة من السعادة

لأن هذه هي الطريقة التي تنظر بها إلى أتعس

Friday Night Friends

Laughing is my twisted way of tears

My mouth turns cries for help into jokes that melt

As solid wall surrenders to the fire and weeps

My ears turn the trauma they've collected into sitcom sketches

for Friday night friends

So they'd slap their knees and curl their eyes

So their foreheads would collapse and their mouths wide

So they'd hold their stomach and clench their fists

It's weird how they look in a moment of happiness

because that's how you look at your saddest

يوم واحد عند الحب

العالم الذي يعيش رأسي فيه يتناقض مع ما تتوقعه عيني

أو أذني تسمع

يحمي رأسي قلبي بالأشياء الحلوة التي تهمس له

لكن لا شيء حلو يظهر منه

أعلم أنني يجب الا أقع في حيلها

لكن عندما يتعلق الأمر بالحب

أصبحت مثل أحمق الفيس

الشخص الذي يتحرك في وقت مبكر جدا

الذي يزين السلة قبل البيض

الذي يكتب النذور قبل الخاتم

الذي يطلب الحلوى قبل المشروبات

في يوم من الأيام سأفعل ذلك بشكل صحيح

دع الحب يتسرّب ببطء

مثل العسل الدافئ في الشاي

ثم ستشعر بتحسن عندما أستعيد بعض الشيء

لقد كنت أعطي الكثير

والقلوب تغضب من الرأس

One Day When Love

The world my head lives in contradicts the one my eyes foresee

or my ears hear

My head protects my heart by the sweet nothings it whispers to

it

But nothing sweet manifests from it

I know I shouldn't fall for her tricks

But when it comes to love

I become like Elvis's fool

The one who moves way too soon

Who decorates the basket before the eggs

Who writes the vows before the ring

Who orders dessert before the drinks

One day I'll do it right

Let the love seep in slowly

Like warm honey in tea

Then it'll feel even better when I get some back

I've been giving too much away

and the hearts getting mad from the head

نجربها مرة أخرى

يشعر شبابي بالضياع عندما أقضيه كلها وأنا صغيرة

لماذا لم نتمكن من إدخار البعض للسنوات الأكبر سنا

ثم يمكن إلقاء اللوم على الأخطاء التي أرتكبها على شيء آخر غيري

يمكن إيواء القبور التي أحفرها مع أي شخص سواي

كم هو مبتذل أن أقول إنني أتمنى أن يعود الوقت إلى الوراء

لذا فإن طفولتي تحدث في مرحلة البلوغ

ثم ستقابل أحلك الأيام بأبري الابتسامات

طيش العقول

ورائحة الجهل المبارك

Let's Try it Again

My youth feels wasted when I spend it all while young

Why couldn't we have saved some for the older years

Then the mistakes I make can be blamed on something other

than me

The graves I dig can be housed with anyone but me

How cliche is it to say I wish time moved backwards

So my childhood occurs in adulthood

Then darkest days will be met with the most innocent of smiles

Mindless of minds

and a smell of blissed ignorance

جامعة لا أحد يهتم

لا يوجد رعب أكبر من مدينة جامعية

الأشخاص مجهولو الهوية الذين تمر بهم إلى المحاضرات الصباحية

إنشاء مساحة محدودة يوم الثلاثاء داخل البار المفضل ليوم الجمعة

ممنوع الدخول مكتوب على عتبة الباب

السنوات التي يجب أن تمر بها

ما مدى رعب الترتيب الزمني

لأن السقوط منه يقود إلى مجهول

لا أحد يريد أن يكتشف

الآمال والأحلام التي بناها الآخرون

عقلك لم يعد وكأنه عقلك بعد الآن

وايامك تحاكي مسجلًا يعزف نفس الأغنية

نحاول الإجبار على المقاطعة لكن عطلات نهاية الأسبوع تقصر

يبدو أن السبيل الوحيد للخروج هو واحد حيث لا أحد يذهب

ما مدى رعب الترتيب الزمني

University of No One Cares

No greater horror than a college town

The faceless people you walk past to AM lectures

Tuesday's creation of liminal space inside Friday's favorite bar

Do Not Enter painted on the doorstep

The years you've got to pass through

How scary is chronological order

Because falling out of it drives an unknown

One no one wants to discover

Hopes and dreams structured by others

Your mind doesn't even feel like yours anymore

And your days mimic a record playing the same song

We try to compel interruption but weekends fall short

Seems the only way out is one where no one is going

How scary is chronological order

بنطال مشتعل

كانت كلماتك عميقة لكن الوعود سطحية

حيث سقط كل حرف في نفس حفرة العدم

لا شيء مغطى بالسكر وترك لي لآكله

صناديق من الورق المقوى مغطاة بورق لامع تحت شجرة بلاستيكية

كل شيء رسمنه كان نابضًا بالحياة ولكن بعد جف صار باهتًا

أتمنى لو كنت أعرف ما سيكون عليه الحال بالفعل

قبل أن يستقر الأمر ولم يكن الأمر كما قلت

كان يجب أن أعرف من الطعم الذي لا معنى له كذبتك الأولى

لكنني أصلحت أخطاءك بأعذاري

حتى أصبحت أعذاري أخطائي

وبينما كان حبي صدفة

شعرت وكأنك لا شيء سوى إزعاج

Liar Liar Pants on Fire

Your words were deep but promises shallow

Where every letter fell down the same hole of nothings

Nothings covered in sugar and left out for me to eat

Cardboard boxes covered in shiny paper under a plastic tree

Everything you painted was vibrant but dried dull

I wish I knew what it was really going to be like

Before it settled in and was nothing like you said it'd be

I should've known from the stale taste of your first lie

But I patched up your mistakes with my excuses

until my excuses became my mistakes

and while my love was a coincidence

Yours felt like nothing but an inconvenience

الرجل الأوسط

لا استطيع ان اكون مترددا الى الابد

في اي وقت ما

شيء يبقى في متناول الجميع

لكن انظر كيف جعلتني اكون

لعب لعبة الانتظار مع شخص أنهى اللعبة

في انتظار دوران الأبواب الخالية من المقابض

لا يمكنني التنافس مع اللامبالاة

Middle Man

I can't be a maybe forever

Or a sometimes whenever

Something kept accessible for whoever

But look how you've made me out to be

Playing a waiting game with someone who finished

Waiting for knobless doors to turn

I can't compete with indifference

لا تلمس موقد ساخن

عندما قالت أمي لا تلمس موقد ساخن

كانت تتحدث إلى قلبك

يمكن ليدك إصلاح خلاياها المكسورة

لكن قلبك لا يستطيع أن يسددقيمة كلماته المسروقة

أو ننسى ذكريات غير مستحقة

كل الطرق التي جذبت الانتباه إليها

الإغراء الذي صنعته

تجاور اللون الأحمر

حيث تكون ساخنة للإغراء

جذابة في التصور

ولكنها قاتلة بلمسة من يد غير متوقعة

Don't Touch a Hot Stove

When mom said don't touch a hot stove

She was speaking to your heart

Your hand can repair its broken cells

But your heart can't repay it's stolen words

Or forget undeserved memories

All the ways you compelled it's attention

The temptation you created

The juxtaposition of red

Where it's hot for temptation

Appealing in visualization

But lethal with a touch of an unexpecting hand

بعد الضوء

بعد أن تحترق الشمعة تترك الغبار ليتحدث عما حدث

بينما كانت الشمعة مشرقة بشكل جميل

الذكريات متروكة في الظلام

والذي يجب أن يتكلم الآن عن النور

ضحية مابعد الحدث

Post Light

After the candle burns it leaves the dust to speak of what

happened

While the candle was beautifully bright

The memories are left in dark

and who must now speak for light

A victim of aftermath

الحب يتسرّب

بطريقة ما لم يكن علي أن أتحدث

لقد سمعوك من خلال كلماتي

بطريقة ما لم يكن علي أن أنظر

لقد رأوك في عيني

شيء لم يكن علي تذوقه

لقد أكلتني بوقتك

في مكان ما لم أضطر للمس

بدلاً من ذلك ، التقى الشعور بشبهة

الحب دائما يتسرب

Love Seeps Through

Somehow I didn't have to speak

They heard you through my words

Somehow I didn't have to look

They saw you in my eyes

Something I didn't have to taste

You ate me with your time

Somewhere I didn't have to touch

The feeling met its match instead

Love *always* seeps through

تخفيضات موسمية

إذا جاء وذهب مثل الصيف

سأفتقده فقط عندما يكون الجو باردًا

إذا ازدهرت في الدفء

سيكون قبيحًا في الشتاء

لا أعرف أبدًا ما إذا كنت سأرتدي سترتي

أو شورت الدينيم الذي أرتديه

إن الضربة القاضية التي تفرضها تناقضاتك قد سلبت الكثير من وقتي

لماذا من الصعب أن تحبني بنفس الطريقة طوال الوقت

سأنتظر حتى تحول الأوراق اللون من أجلك

لكنك مثل الطيور تطير إلى مناخات أكثر حرارة

عندما تصبح هشة وباردة

أظن أنني سأبقى بعد ذلك

انتظر الشمس أن تشرق

تتحمل ما لن تتحمله

العشب أكثر اخضرارا على الجانب الآخر

أيا كان الجانب

What's Left of Me

Seasonal Sale

If it came and went like summer

I'll only miss it when it's cold

If it blossomed in the warmth

It'll be ugly when it's winter

I never know wether to put my jacket on

Or my cut off denim shorts

The whiplash your inconsistencies compel have stolen too much

of my time

Why's it so hard to love me the same all the time

I'd wait for the leaves to turn color for you

But like birds you fly to hotter climates

When this one becomes brittle and cold

I guess I'll stay then

Wait for the sun to come out

Endure what you won't

The grass is greener on the other side

Whichever side your not on

المفقود

الحياة لا تريدنا أن نجد معناها

ستجدها بنفسها

لديك اليوم

تذكر الأمس

نأمل أن يكون هناك غدًا

Lost But Don't Find

Life doesn't need us to find it's meaning

It'll find it itself

Have today

Remember yesterday

and hope there's tomorrow

البيوت

لقد صنعت لك منزلًا

كل القصص المروية

، والكتابة المستقبلية

لقد وضعت الطوب حولك

وسقف فوقك

لذلك في أي طقس سأجدك

لا يزال قائما

ولكن عندما جاء المطر

لم يعودوا هناك

الآن أنظر إلى حقل فارغ

بشكل كهف فيه

من حيث كنت ذات مرة

المساحة التي شغلتها

لذلك نثرت البذور

والوقت الذي ضيعته

في نمو البذرة

Real Estate

I made a home of you

All the told stories

and future writing,

I placed bricks around you

and a roof over you

So in whatever weather I'd find you

Still standing

But when the rain came

you weren't there anymore

Now I look at an empty field

With a shape caved in

Of where you once were

The space you took up

So I planted seeds

and the time I wasted

is used in my growth

The seed

مسألة عائلية

يبدو أن الجميع يعرف الا انت

أو كنت تعرف ولكن لم ترغب في أن يعرف الجميع

نأسف هو ابن عم الرفض وقد دعاني إلى لم الشمل

وأنا أقف مكتوف الأيدي أمام سوء حظهم

Family Affair

Seemed like everyone knew but you

Or you knew but didn't want everyone to

Regret's the cousin of rejection and it's invited me to the

reunion

As I stand idle to their misfortune

مجموعتي

بطريقة ما الحب يهدئ العالم من حولنا

إن تثبيت مثل هذا الكيان الفردي يخلق عزلة صامتة

إنه حلو ومر

سأصب كل انتباهي عليك

بينما أشاهدك تلفت الانتباه إلى الأشخاص من حولك

كأنني أجمع القمامة التي ترميها كلما تذهب

تلك التي ستطلبها لاحقًا

كم هو مناسب لك

كم هي يائسة مني

My Collection

Somehow love quiets the world around us

The fixation of such a single entity creates silent loneliness

It's bittersweet

I'd pour all my attention into you

As I watch you throw yours to the people around you

Like I'm collecting the litter you drop as you go

The ones you'd ask for later

How convenient for you

How desperate of me

كابوس الضواحي

سأعيش الحياة التي أخافها إذا كان ذلك يعني أنك ستكون فيها

ستكون أقل رعبا

الرقص حول موائد العشاء المكدسة بالفواتير

سادق سياج الاعتصام الابيض

أنت فقط تحصل على الجانب الآخر منه

سأعمل على أن أكون معك منذ الخامسة وحتي التاسعة

وبعد أن نحدق بصراحة في بقية الحياة ، لا نعرف كيف نعيش

حتى نموت

على الأقل سنفعل ذلك معًا أيضًا

Suburban Nightmare

I'd live the life I fear if it meant you'd be in it

It'll be less scary

Dancing around dinner tables stacked with bills

I'd hammer down the white picket fence

You just get on the other side of it

The 9-5 I'd work to be with you for the 5-9

and after we'd stare blankly at the rest of the life we don't know

how to live

Until we die

At least we'd do that together too

طاب مساؤك

أنا ضحية للشعور بالذنب الذي ينبض بالحياة مع أنفاس القمر

لأن السماء المظلمة لا تمنحك الكثير لتتطلع إليه

لذلك عليك أن تنظر في الداخل

وتجد حذر حياتك

اعضاء مهتزة لا يمكن التنبؤ به

الذنب وحش الظلام

لذلك تتوسل خطوة إلى الوراء

لتغيير أفعال ماضيك

لكن حتى بالأمس ، كان القمر حياً

لا جدوى من محاولة الهروب من الليل

Goodnight

I'm victim to the guilt that comes alive with the breath of the moon

because dark skies don't give you much to look out to

So you'd look inside

and find the wary of your life

Shaking organs with unpredictable tomorrow's

Guilt is a monster of the dark

So you pled for a step backward

To change the actions of your past

But even yesterday, the moon was alive

No point in trying to escape the night

من وماذا وأين

عالق في بغالبه

لا تصل أبدًا إلى مكان ما

ودائما لا تصل إلى أي مكان

دائما ما تكون شيئًا

وأبدا أن أكون كل شيء

ثم للجميع

لقد أصبحت شخصًا صادف أن تكون كذلك

Who, What, Where

Stuck in the almost

is never getting somewhere

and always getting nowhere

It's always being something

and never being everything

Then to everyone

You've become someone who happened to be

قطعة قطعة

لقد جئت من أجزاء من كل الأشياء التي أحببتها

، وجميع الأماكن التي رأيتها

كل الموسيقى التي سمعتها

والمحادثات التي كنت أتوق إلى إعادة إحيائها

Piece by Piece

I come from fragments of all the things I've loved

and all the places I've seen,

All the music I've heard

and conversations I've longed to relive

بكاء

طعم ابتسامتك مر

ولكن ليس هناك ما هو أسوأ من دمعتك

المسارات المظلمة التي يتركها وراءه

لتلطيخ الخدود التي ابتسمت ذات مرة

Cry

The aftertaste of your smile is bitter

But nothing is worse than your tear

The dark tracks it leaves behind

To stain the cheeks that once smiled

شمس و قمر

أقول للشمس أني أفتقدك

إنها الوحيدة التي ترا كلانا

أود أن أعتقد أنك تتحدث معها أيضًا

لذا فهي تاتي القمر لتحمل أعبائنا

ويحتفظ بها حتى تستجيب

أو حتى تعود

أيهما يحدث أولاً

Sun and Moon

I tell the sun I miss you

She's the only one that sees us both

I'd like to think you talk to her too

So she sets the moon to carry our burdens

and holds it safe until you respond

Or until she comes back

Whichever happens first

لحظات وذكريات

أنا مغرم باللحظات

لأن هذا عندما تفكر بي

أشعر بالغيرة من الذكريات

لأن هذا كل ما عليك التفكير فيه

Moments and Memories

I'm fond of the moments

because that's when you think of me

I'm jealous of the memories

because that's all you have to think of me

افتقدني

أنا أفتقدك أكثر في الأماكن التي لم نذهب إليها أبدًا

والصور التي لم نلتقطها قط

الان اسمعك من صوت ذاكرتي

الأوهام تبقيك على قيد الحياة في العالم الذي أصنعه

تجلت المساحة التي كنت تشغلها في ظل يتتبعني

Miss Me Nots

I miss you most in the places we never went

And the pictures we never took

Now I hear you from the voice of my memory

Delusions keep you alive in the world I create

The space you'd occupy has manifested into a shadow that trails

me

What's Left of Me

Nora Yasier Elsayed

Your name is written on every award I win

announced on every stage I cross

and recognized in every ceremony I attend

Yasier Elsayed

For every recognition you championed the path to get there

I celebrate every material success won by your invisible sacrifice

through the name I proudly carry

What follows Nora is Yasier Elsayed

What made Nora is Yasier Elsayed

I hope to land on the worlds greatest stage

Just to hear your name announced again

In my death they'll print us both on my cement tomb

So every thought and prayer is gone to you too

A thousand words won't speak to the happiness you've touched

me with

A thousand photos won't picture the smile you forged on me

every day

To the world it's Yasier Elsayed

To me, its Baba

What's Left of Me

نورا ياسر السيد

اسمك مكتوب على كل جائزة فزت بها

أعلن في كل مرحلة أعبرها

وتقدير في كل احتفال أحضره

ياسر السيد

لكل اعتراف ، دافعت عن الطريق للوصول إلى هناك

أحتفل بكل نجاح مادي حققته تضحيتك غير المرئية من خلال الاسم الذي أحمله بكل فخر

ما يلي نورا هو ياسر السيد

ما صنع نورا هو ياسر السيد

آمل أن أهبط على أعظم مسرح في العالم

فقط لسماع اسمك يعلن مرة أخرى

في موتي سيطبعوننا كلانا على شواهد قبري الاسمنتية

لذا فإن كل ذكر ودعاء تذهب إليك أيضًا

ألف كلمة لن تعبر عن السعادة التي غمرتني بها

ألف صورة لن تصور الابتسامة التي ترسمها في حياتي

What's Left of Me

للعالم إنه ياسر السيد

بالنسبة لي ، إنه بابا

Our College Home

The subliminal nature of the college home

where we all are in life's waiting room

Four walls and four of us

We'd push them outward as we grow

The laughter of our Saturday night 20s

and the quiet of our Sunday night clean up

Burnt pans and forgotten dishes compel metaphors for our mistakes

Awoken by the school bell and asleep by the wonders of the world

One of us might solve it soon and one of us might find another one soon

God I'd miss the collective field we played on

The illusion of reality we lived in

The innocence of adulthood we proclaimed

But the ignorance we soon dismantled

Our college home carried out the childhood playground games

Our college home cut us a slice of the world

But disguised it with sweet surroundings and filled it with dreams

Soon our college home will go 4 separate ways

Our college home will turn into where we went not where we are

Where we've been and look at us now

Our college home

ارجع

لوني الأزرق هو ظل لك

أصبحت المساحة التي ملأتها فارغة

وكرسيك الذي جلست عليه قد انهار

لا يمكننا التعرف على ذكرياتنا بدونك

الآن نرقص حول نفاد صبرنا مع مرور الوقت

حتى نعيدك

وأتوسل إلى الزمن لترجع

Come Back

What colors me blue is the shadow of you

The space you filled has become hollow

and the chair you sat in has caved in

We can't recognize our memories without you

Now we dance around our impatience with time

Until we get you back

and beg for it to rewind

باقي الكتابة

الشعراء الأموات لم يعودوا يكتبون في الجنة

الأسئلة التي نتألم للإجابة عليها تكمن الي أين نحن ذاهبون

الوقت الذي نفكر فيه

الحب الذي نسأله

الحزن الذي نحمله

السعادة التي نضيعها

سرعان ما يتم العثور على الضائع هناك

موتي الشعراء مع من جعلهم شعراء

ومن قتلهم

موتي الشعراء في الجنة متبادلين

نعطي وتعطي

لا يستطيع الشعراء الميتون أن يتكلموا بالمجاز لأنه سيصبح حقيقة

الشعراء الأموات ، سأراكم قريبا

Rest in Writing

Dead poets write no longer in heaven

The questions we ache to answer lie where we are going

The time we ponder

The love we question

The grief we hold

The happiness we slip away

That who is lost is soon found there

Dead poets heaven is with who made them a poet

and who killed them

Dead poets heaven is reciprocal

We give and it gives

Dead poets can't speak a metaphor as it'll grow into fruition

Dead poets, I'll see you soon

عزيزتي ، لقد قلصت حبنا

انظر إلى ذرة الغبار التي صنعتها لنا

المحادثات الآن مجرد رسائل

الذكريات الآن مجرد لحظات

الحب الآن مجرد صداقة

سأعيش فيه وحدي

أسهب في الحديث عنها لفترة أطول

أتساءل كيف يمكن لشخص ما أن يكون بهذه القسوة

كيف يمكن لشخص ما تقصير العاطفة والضغط على الروح

هذا عندما ما تفعله

يعبر عما ستفعل

Honey, I Shrunk Our Love

Look at the speck of dust you've shrunken us too

Conversations now just letters

Memories now just moments

Love now just an acquaintanceship

I'll just live in it alone

Dwell on it longer

Wonder how someone can be so cruel

How someone can shorten a passion and squeeze a soul

This is when what you do

Speaks for what you'll do

افطر

أنا أميل نفسي لأصب فيك

مثل قهوة الإفطار أو شاي بعد الظهر

جئت في راحتك واختلطت مع رغباتك

كريم وسكر لملء العيوب

إناء نصف فارغ

بينما يتوسل لي الأسف ألا أقوم بنفس الخطأ مرتين

Break your Fast

I tilted myself to pour into you

Like breakfast coffee or afternoon tea

I came in your convenience and mixed with your desires

Cream and sugar to fill the bitter imperfections

My pot's become half empty

While regret begs me not to make the same mistake twice

اليوم أنا وغدا سأفعل

حضرت اليوم جنازتك مرتدية مليون تابوت

كل الناس كانت من أجلك

عاشق تحول إلى صديق أجبر غريبًا

لقد قاموا بلفك بقطعة قماش مخملية

لقد سحبته مرة أخرى لإلقاء نظرة أخيرة

ما رأيته كان لون بشرتك وردية اللون

الشباب في جسدك يذكرني

الأيام التي سأعود إليها

سرعان ما انقطعت الفكرة واستدرت

لمواجهة بقية الأيام التي تنتظرني

قبل أن أرتدي المخمل وأحمر الخدود باللون الوردي

Today I and Tomorrow I'll

Today I attended your funeral dressed in a million caskets

All the people I was to you

A *lover* turned *friend* forced *stranger*

They had you draped in velvet cloth

I pulled it back to take one last look

What I saw was your skin blushed pink

The youth in your body reminds me

Of the days I'd go back to

Soon the thought was interrupted and I turned around

To face the rest of the days that await me

Before I'm wrapped in velvet and blush in pink

الحب الذي زرعته

هل أنت النبات الذي سقيته كثيرًا؟

أو

الذي وضعته في الشمس لفترة طويلة؟

هل هذا هو السبب في أنك ذبلت وفقدت لونك؟

أفتقد كيف كنت عندما رأيتك لأول مرة

عندما تعرفت عليك

حمل اللون الأخضر الخاص بك الدهشة

الآن أنت شاحب مثقل بماضينا

تمنيت لو احتفظت ببعض الماء في إناء

وحفظت بعض الشمس لبشرتي

The Love I Gardened

Are you the plant I watered too often

or

kept in the sun too long?

Is that why you withered down and lost your color?

I miss how you were when I first saw you

When I got to know you

Your green carried excitement

Now you're pale burdened with our past

I wish I had kept some water in my pot

and saved the sun for my skin

23 يناير

يدك الملتفة حول يدي تحدثت بمليون كلمة كنت أعرف أنك ستقولها

بالنسبة لي ، كانت كل حركة موازية لتلك التي اعتدت القيام بها

الضحك الذي اعتدت أن يكون لديك

الابتسامة التي اعتدت حملها

لم يمر وقت وأنت غير موجود

لكن بقربك شعرت أن العالم يتحرك بجانبي

شعرت بالثواني عدت و الدقائق

حتى النهاية شعرت قدمي بأنها ملتصقة بالبلاط المرقط

حتى قمت بلف يدي وكنت أنا وأنت مرة أخرى

سمعته من قبل مليون مرة ولكن اليوم كان لديه ضوء لم يسبق له مثيل

حملت عبارة "أنا أحبك" ثقلًا لم أكن أعرف أنني سأحمله

شعرت وكأن كل يوم مضى منكمش في تلك الذاكرة

وقلّد الهواء الصدمة في الغرفة

وقفت ساكنة وشاهدتك تفعل ذلك مرة أخرى

لا تصمد المعجزات فقط عندما تتنفس الحياة من خلالها

فجاءوا بمجرد دعوتهم

What's Left of Me

January 23rd

Your hand wrapped around mine spoke a million words I knew you'd say

To me, every movement paralleled the ones you used to do

The laughs you used to have

The smile you used to hold

No time passed when you're not around

But by you I felt the world move alongside me

I felt the seconds and counted the minutes

Until the very end my feet felt glued to the speckled tiles

Until I wrapped my hand and it was just me and you again

I heard it a million times prior but today it had a light like never before

I love you carried a weight I didn't know I'd hold

It felt like every past day shrunk into that memory

and the air mimicked the shock in the room

It stood still and watched you do it again

Miracles only hold when life breathes through them

and they came as soon as you called upon them

سنوات المراهقة

أتمنى لو جمعت سنوات المراهقة التي تخلصت منها

تلك التي تخليت عنها من أجلنا

وأتمنى أن أعيدهم الآن عندما تكون في أمس الحاجة إليهم

عندما يفرغ المنزل وأنت تجلس نادما عل ما فات

كيف كانت الحياة مع عائلتك ،

تلك التي تركتها لنا

ما هي الحياة التي كنت ستعيشها بدون الأميال التي سافرت إليها للوصول إلى هنا

المنزل الذي تركته لبناء واحد هنا

الأطفال الثلاثة الذين أعطيتهم سنواتك أيضًا

لقد ذهب كل هذا الآن

أنت تنظر إلى السنوات التي تركتها

وأتمنى أن تعرف أين تنفقه

في بلد لم تعرفه أو بلد لا تعرفه الآن

أين منزلك عندما يصبح الناس غير معروفين؟

عندما كان الوقت طويلاً للعودة إليه؟

هل تطارد سنوات المراهقة تلك

ام تموت غارقا في دموع مراهقتك؟

What's Left of Me

Teenage Years

I wish I could collect the teenage years you threw away

the ones you gave up for us

and I wish to have returned them now when you need them most

When the house is empty and you sit with your delayed regret

What life would've been with your family,

the ones you left for us

What could've been without the miles you flew to get here

The house you left to build here

The three kids you gave your years too

That are now all gone

You look at the years you have left

and wish you knew where to spend it

In a country you didn't know or a country you now don't know

Where's home for you when the people become unrecognizable?

When it's been too long for you to go back to?

Do you chase those teenage years

or die drowning in your teenage tears?

قصيدة للأماكن التي زرتها

شعرت شمس إسبانيا بالدفء

شعرت مياه إيطاليا بالبرودة

شعرت رمال المغرب بالنعومة

شعرت قمر فرنسا أكثر إشراقا

كانت أشجار بلجيكا أكثر اكتمالا

كانت الصخور الألمانية أصعب

كان عشب دبي أكثر خضرة

وكان سكان بالي أقل رشاقة

شعرت سنغافورة بحلاوة الطعام

شعرت هواء هولندا أنظف

شعرت جزر تايلاند بأنها أكبر

في كل مكان أصبحت فيه أحدث

في كل ثقافة كنت أشعر بالانعكاس

Ode to the Places I've Been

The sun of Spain felt warmer

The water of Italy felt cooler

The sand of Morocco felt softer

The moon of France felt brighter

The Belgium trees were fuller

The German rocks were harder

Dubai's grass was greener

and Bali's people were leaner

The food of Singapore felt sweeter

The air of Holland felt cleaner

The islands of Thailand felt larger

In every place I became newer

In every culture I felt mirrored

لوحتي

دخلت في حرب مع الفنانة التي رسمتني

كرهت الألوان التي اختاروها

أشفق على الألوان التي اختاروها

أضع اللوم على لوح الألوان

وفضلت عدم ائتماني عندما جلبت لي الحظ السعيد

في عزلة ، بدات أنها مصدر كل الشرور

لكن عندما أحبطت بالغرام ، تنفست

My Canvas

I fought in a war with the artist that painted me

I hated the colors they chose

I *pitied* the colors they chose

I put the blame on the palette

and favored it no credit when it brought me good fortunate

In isolation it seemed to be the source of all evil

But when surrounded I dug into the pride it beamed

ورقة بيضاء صارخة

أتساءل عما إذا كنت أعطي هذه الكلمات أكثر من اللازم

إذا كنت أكتب أكثر مما أقوله

هل هناك إهمال في طريقة حديثي معك

لأنني دونتها كلها بدلاً من ذلك

الأمر أسهل بكثير

لتتخيل وجهك كالورقة البيضاء الصارخة

بدلا من حق أمامي

أعتقد أنه سينتهي بي الأمر لاقول أقل من ذلك بكثير

ويخدمك ظلم

عندما يمكنني الكتابة فقط بدلا من ذلك

وسوف تقرأ ما لا يمكنني قوله

Stark White Paper

I wonder if I give these words too much

If I'm writing more than I'm saying

Is there neglect in the way I speak to you

because I wrote it all down instead

It's just so much easier

to imagine your face as the stark white paper

rather than right in front of me

I think I'd end up saying much less

and serve you an injustice

When instead I can just write

and you'll read what I could never say

يوم ما

يوما ما يمكننا الجلوس في نفس الغرفة

نسترجع كل الوقت الضائع

سأرسم لك القصص التي أردت أن أخبرك بها

وسوف ترسم لي الطريق الذي سلكته

أسمع ما إذا كانت أحلام الملعب تحققت

ام الأوهام التي أطعمتها أصبحت واقعك

أضحك على الأخطاء وأغلق الأبواب

لكن تبعث بفخر الإنجازات والنجاحات

أراقب وجهك عندما أصبح كل ما تريدني أن أصبح

ثم استدر الأمل أن نرى بعضنا البعض مرة أخرى في يوم ما

One Day

One day we can sit in the same room

and call back all the time we missed

I'll paint you the stories I wanted to tell you

and you'll draw me the path you went through

I get to hear if the playground dreams manifested

or the delusions I fed became your reality

I get to laugh at the mistakes and shut doors

But beam with pride at the accomplishes and successes

I get to watch your face when all you wanted me to become, became

Then turn around and hope we see each other again some other day

نورا ونورا

في لغتي الإنجليزية ، أنا نورا ، أنا أمريكية ، أنا سوداء ، أنا طالبة جامعية ، أنا أمي وأبي ، أبلغ من العمر 18 عامًا وأخرج من المنزل ، أنا أنا كسر القالب ، أنا من ، ESOL برجر بالجبن وبطاطا مقلية ، انا الجيل الأول ، أنا ثنائية الجوازات ، أنا محظوظة ، لقد نجحت ، أنا ليبرالي ، لقد ، iMessage أنا Gen-Z ، استيقظت ، أنا سحر الفتاة السوداء ، أنا تسربت الشيك ، أنا مصافحة ولست متأكدًا من أنا

في لغتي العربية أنا نورا ، أنا عربية ، أنا أفريقي ، أنا فول مدمس ، أنا زيت زيتون ، أنا صوت العود في الصباح ، أنا ماما وبابا ، أنا أنا بخور من رقائق الخشب ، أنا مليون أبناء عمومة ، أنا مجموعة محادثات أنا قهوة وشاي بالنعناع غارقة في السكر ، أنا مجوهرات ، WhatsApp العين الشريرة ، أنا الأهرامات ، أنا النيل ، أنا لوحات اسم ذهبية ، أنا ما شاء الله وإن شاء الله ، أنا قبلات على كل خد ، أنا مغطاة بالحناء ، وأنا واثق جدًا من أنا

Nora and Noura

In my English I'm Nora, I'm American, I'm Black, I'm a University student, I'm mom and dad, I'm 18 and out the house, I'm cheeseburgers and fries, I'm ESOL classes, I'm breaking the mold, I'm first generation, I'm two passports, I'm privileged, I'm 'made it out', I'm liberal, I'm woke, I'm black girl magic, I'm Gen-Z, I'm iMessage, I'm spilt the check, I'm handshakes and not sure who I am

In my Arabic I'm Noura, I'm Arab, I'm African, I'm fava beans, I'm olive oil, I'm the sound of the oud in the morning, I'm Mama and Baba, I'm incense from wood chips, I'm a million cousins, I'm WhatsApp group chats, I'm jabena and mint tea soaked in sugar, I'm evil eye jewelry, I'm pyramids, I'm the Nile, I'm gold name plates, I'm MashAllahs and InshAllahs, I'm kisses on each cheek, I'm henna covered arms, and so sure in who I am

في ذرة

في الظلام وجدت ذرة منك

واحتفظت بها حتى غرست أظافري في جلدي

دم مغلف بالمعدن يقطر من حزنا

من الوقت الضائع

إنها تحافظ على نفسها ملطخة الآن

لوحة خلدت على جسد ستزول قريباً

هذا كل ما هو حقا وصمة عار

In a Speck

In the darkness I found a speck of you

and held it until my nails dug into my skin

Metallic coated blood dripped down in grief

of the time we missed

It keeps itself a stain now

A painting immortalized on a body soon to be gone

That's all stains really are

بيت الدموع

كما لو كان الموت قد شعر بأنه أكبر ألم في العالم

أو فضاءات مظلمة ، محيطات عميقة ، أماكن غريبة

إذن لم تقابل قط الدموع المنهمرة على خد أمهات

إنها تعيش فوق عظام وجنتيها مباشرة

لا تسقط ابدا من ابواب قوتها

الأم تحمل البيت على وجهها

وإذا سقطت الدمعة

فاض المنزل

لا تترك أي شيء في أثرها

Housed Tears

As if dying felt like the world's greatest pain

or dark spaces, deep oceans, strange places

Then you've never met the teardrops housed on a mothers cheek

They live right above her cheekbones

Never falling past the gates of her strength

The mother holds the home in her face

and if the tear falls

The home floods

To leave nothing in its trace

عشرون شيئًا

لا شيء يتغير حقًا سوى الأشخاص المحيطين بكعكتك

سوف يتبادلون الدخول والخروج قبل أن تلاحظ ذلك حقًا

ثم ستجد نفسك وحيدًا تمامًا

وتصبح متفرجًا على أخطائك

حتى لا يمكنك التعرف على نفسك بعد الآن

من هو هذا الغريب الذي يرقد في سريري معي

هذا الآن يشارك في نفس المقعد مثلي

لا تقلق

فقط أغلق عيناك

وتمنى أمنية

ربما العام القادم سيكون مختلف

Twenty Somethings

Nothing really changes but the people surrounding your cake

They'll swap in and out before you even really notice

Then you'll find yourself all alone

and become a bystander to your own faults

Until you can't recognize yourself anymore

Who is this stranger that lays in my bed with me

That now shares the same seat as me

Don't worry

Just close your eyes

and make a wish

Maybe next year it will be different

الغضب في فضاء الحب

في مواجهة الغضب ، يقشعر جلدي للخلف

لتكشف عن العظام التي بقيت تعتني بك

علمت يومًا ما أنك ستشتاق إلي

في ضباب النظرات عبر الغرفة

كنت ستدرك أنه لم يعد كافيا بعد الآن

كنت ستبحث عن طريقة للزواج بين المسافة بيننا ،

اجمعهما معًا مرة أخرى

لإحياء المحادثات التي أجريناها ذات مرة

كل هذا أثناء تواجدها بعيدًا

Anger in the Space of Love

In the face of anger my skin peeled back

to reveal the bones that remained to care for you

I knew someday you'd long for me

in the mist of glances across the room

You'd realize it wasn't enough anymore

You'd look for a way to marry the space between us,

bring them back together again

To revive the conversations we once had

All while she's away

ماريتا

، أعدني إلى أتلانتا

مباشرة الي ماريتا

سافرنا على طريق الأحد السريع

بحثنا عنك في انعكاس الماء

مباشرة بعد دموعنا غمرة سيارتنا

عندما لونت أضواء الشوارع كل قطرة

Marietta

Take me back to Atlanta,

right to Marietta's

On Sunday's highway we drove

We looked for you in the reflection of the water

right after our tears dressed our car

While the streets lights colored each drop

ميلاد الفكرة

أفضل نصيحة قدمتها لك

ولدت من أسوأ الأخطاء

سأختبئ عنك

The Birth of Advice

The best advice I gave to you

was birthed from the worst mistakes

I'll hide from you

ستارة مغلقة

وبعد ذلك يضرب رأسي الوسادة
وألقي نظرة على مروحة السقف
ينغلق بابي وتنخفت الأضواء

انتهت العروض في النهاية

أخلع الزي وأحفظ سيناريو الغد
الألوان التي رسمتها تفسد وتكشف بشرتي
أستطيع أخيرًا أن أحس بالريح
وبعد ذلك يلتقي الحزن بالوسادة

Closed Curtain

And then my head hits the pillow

and I look at the ceiling fan

My door closes and lights dim

The shows finally over

I strip off the costume and save tomorrows script

The colors I painted rub off and bare dresses my skin

I can finally feel the wind

and then the sorrow meets the pillow

أستثنائي

بعض الأشياء التي يجب أن أفعلها لنفسي

وبعض الأشياء التي سأحتفظ بها لنفسي

إلى الاستثنائي في داخلي أتوسل لخروجه مني

شاهدني أنشر حياتي في مكتبة الأحلام

سوف تسقط من الأرض إلى السقف ثم تبقي ليقرأها من يأتون بعدي

Extraordinary

Some things I have to do for myself

and some things I'd keep to myself

To the extraordinary in me begging for its way out

Watch me self publish my life into a library of dreams

It'll fall from floor to ceiling then left to be read by those who come after me

www.ingramcontent.com/pod-product-compliance
Lightning Source LLC
Chambersburg PA
CBHW020248010526
44107CB00002B/152